T0400639

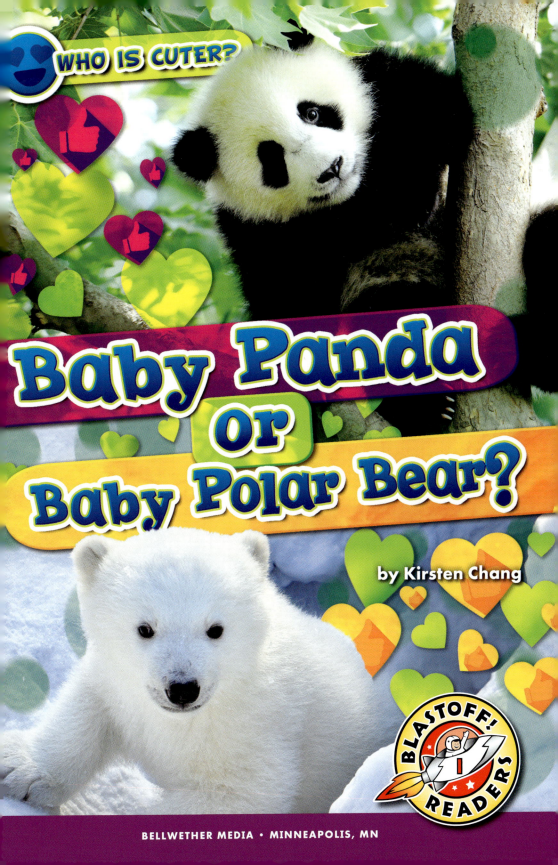

Baby Panda
or
Baby Polar Bear?

by Kirsten Chang

BLASTOFF! READERS

BELLWETHER MEDIA • MINNEAPOLIS, MN

Blastoff! Readers are carefully developed by literacy experts to build reading stamina and move students toward fluency by combining standards-based content with developmentally appropriate text.

Level 1 provides the most support through repetition of high-frequency words, light text, predictable sentence patterns, and strong visual support.

Level 2 offers early readers a bit more challenge through varied sentences, increased text load, and text-supportive special features.

Level 3 advances early-fluent readers toward fluency through increased text load, less reliance on photos, advancing concepts, longer sentences, and more complex special features.

★ **Blastoff! Universe**

Reading Level

Grade **K**

Grades **1–3**

Grade **4**

This edition first published in 2025 by Bellwether Media, Inc.

No part of this publication may be reproduced in whole or in part without written permission of the publisher. For information regarding permission, write to Bellwether Media, Inc., Attention: Permissions Department, 6012 Blue Circle Drive, Minnetonka, MN 55343.

Library of Congress Cataloging-in-Publication Data

LC record for Baby Panda or Baby Polar Bear? available at: https://lccn.loc.gov/2024035004

Editor: Rachael Barnes • Designer: Brittany McIntosh

Printed in the United States of America, North Mankato, MN.

Table of Contents

Baby Cubs

Baby pandas and baby polar bears are both called cubs.

panda
cub

polar bear
cub

5

Both baby bears have short tails. They are cute **mammals**!

short tail

Black and White

Panda cubs have black and white fur. Polar bear cubs have white fur.

Panda cubs have wide, flat noses. Polar bear cubs have round noses.

round
nose

Polar bear cubs have huge paws to swim. Panda cubs have special paws to hold **bamboo**.

swimming

bamboo

13

Homes in Trees and Snow

Panda cubs sleep
in tree **dens**.
Polar bear cubs
sleep in snow dens.

tree
den

snow den

15

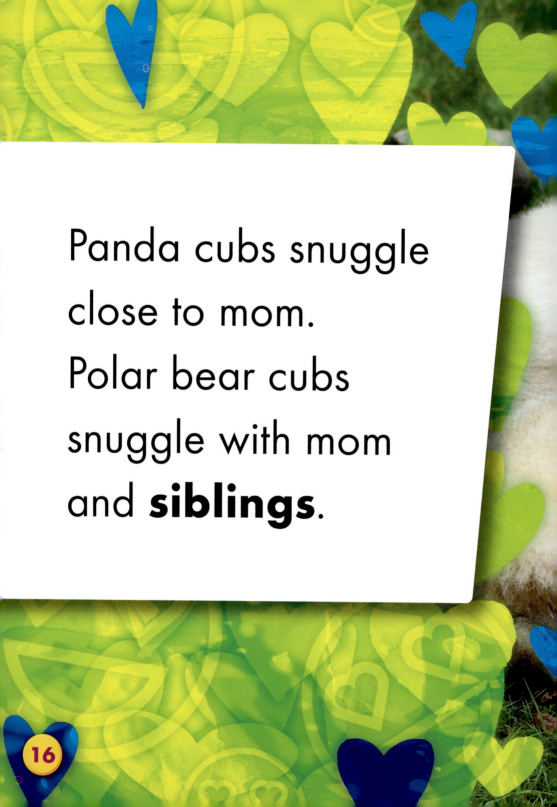

Panda cubs snuggle close to mom. Polar bear cubs snuggle with mom and **siblings**.

siblings
with mom

17

Panda cubs
squeal and bark!
Polar bear cubs hum.
Who is cuter?

Who Is Cuter?

wide, flat nose

black and white fur

special paws

Baby Panda

holds bamboo

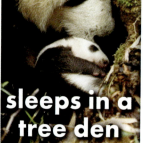

sleeps in a tree den

snuggles with mom

round nose

white fur

huge paws

Baby Polar Bear

swims

sleeps in a snow den

snuggles with mom and siblings

21

Glossary

bamboo

a tall, tree-like grass that grows in warm places

siblings

brothers and sisters

dens

sheltered places

mammals

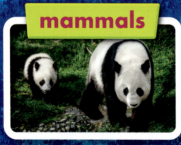

warm-blooded animals that have backbones and feed their young milk

To Learn More

AT THE LIBRARY

Bowman, Chris. *Giant Pandas*. Minneapolis, Minn.: Bellwether Media, 2025.

Rathburn, Betsy. *Baby Pandas*. Minneapolis, Minn.: Bellwether Media, 2022.

Sanderson, Whitney. *Meet a Baby Polar Bear*. Minneapolis, Minn.: Lerner Publications, 2024.

ON THE WEB

FACTSURFER

Factsurfer.com gives you a safe, fun way to find more information.

1. Go to www.factsurfer.com.

2. Enter "baby panda or baby polar bear" into the search box and click 🔍.

3. Select your book cover to see a list of related content.

Index

The images in this book are reproduced through the courtesy of: Hupeng | Dreamstime.com, front cover (panda); evaurban, front cover (polar bear), pp. 5 (polar bear cub), 9; Eric Isselee, pp. 3, 20 (panda), 21 (polar bear); Alatom, pp. 4-5; Alexey Seafarer, pp. 6-7; Wonderly Imaging, p. 7; Bbu Kurkovva, pp. 8-9; AndreAnita, pp. 10-11, 21 (snuggles with mom and siblings); Foreverhappy, pp. 11, 20 (holds bamboo); ian cruickshank/ Alamy, pp. 12-13; imageBROKER.com GmbH & Co. KG/ Alamy, p. 13 (swimming); Richard Wear/ Design Pics/ Getty Images, pp. 14-15; Keren Su/China Span/ Alamy, p. 15 (tree den); yanmiao, pp. 16-17; isabel kendzior, p. 17 (siblings with mom), 22 (siblings); Perky Pets/ Alamy, pp. 18-19; SuperStock/ Mitsuaki Iwago/ Minden Pictures, p. 20 (sleeps in tree dens); GM Photo Images/ Alamy, p. 21 (swims); Jenny E. Ross, p. 21 (sleeps in snow dens); Tupungato, p. 22 (bamboo); Elena Birkina, p. 22 (dens); Hung Chung Chih, p. 22 (mammals).